CLOUD

MARY MAGDALENE
Apostle to the Apostles

Dinah Chapman Simmons

Little Rock
Scripture Study

A ministry of the Diocese of Little Rock
in partnership with Liturgical Press

Nihil obstat: Jerome Kodell, OSB, *Censor Librorum.*
Imprimatur: ✛ Anthony B. Taylor, Bishop of Little Rock, July 13, 2018.

Cover design by Ann Blattner. Photo courtesy of Lightstock. Used with permission.

Photos/illustrations: Pages 8, 12, 14, 17, 19, 23, 27, 29, 31, 34, 38, 40, 44, Getty Images. Used with permission.

ISBN: 978-0-8146-4414-0 (print); 978-0-8146-4439-3 (ebook)

Contents

Introduction

Alive in the Word brings you resources to deepen your understanding of Scripture, offer meaning for your life today, and help you to pray and act in response to God's word.

Use any volume of **Alive in the Word** in the way best suited to you.

- **For individual learning and reflection,** consider this an invitation to prayerfully journal in response to the questions you find along the way. And be prepared to move from head to heart and then to action.
- **For group learning and reflection,** arrange for three sessions where you will use the material provided as the basis for faith sharing and prayer. You may ask group members to read each chapter in advance and come prepared with questions answered. In this kind of session, plan to be together for about an hour. Or, if your group prefers, read and respond to the questions together without advance preparation. With this approach, it's helpful to plan on spending more time for each group session in order to adequately work through each of the chapters.

- **For a parish-wide event or use within a larger group,** provide each person with a copy of this volume, and allow time during the event for quiet reading, group discussion and prayer, and then a final commitment by each person to some simple action in response to what he or she learned.

This volume on the topic of Mary Magdalene explores her role as the first to proclaim the resurrection of Jesus and is one of several volumes dedicated to **Cloud of Witnesses**. The pages of our Bibles are filled with the stories of women and men who have played a unique role in salvation history. By entering into a few key biblical passages written by or describing these people, we begin to see how our own story continues God's great work of salvation in the world. Their witness, handed on to us from centuries ago, continues to speak to us and challenge us to stand as faithful witnesses in today's world.

Prologue

Mary Magdalene is named more than a dozen times in the four gospels—more than any other woman and more than most men, even most of the Twelve Apostles! And, as Peter's name heads the lists of male followers of Jesus, Mary Magdalene's name almost invariably heads lists of women followers. It seems reasonable to conclude that she was well known and well respected in the early church.

The gospels place Mary Magdalene among the disciples involved in Jesus' public ministry and also tell us of her presence at the cross and at the empty tomb. She was probably one of the group of women gathered together with Jesus' male disciples on Pentecost, as described in Acts, although the only woman actually named in that passage is Mary of Nazareth (Acts 1:14). Her part in Jesus' story spans the public ministry to Pentecost (and no doubt beyond).

Most of what we know about Mary Magdalene comes from the passion and resurrection narratives. Surely, her great Easter morning proclamation—"I have seen the Lord!"—is the reason her name has been remembered throughout Christian history. With these words, Mary Magdalene became the first of Jesus' followers to proclaim the good news of the resurrection to other followers. It is this role as messenger of the good news on Easter Sunday that earned her the ancient title "apostolorum apostola"—"the apostle to the apostles."

But Mary was part of the story of Jesus well before the resurrection. We know that she was present during his public ministry, and she was present at his crucifixion. This abiding presence is an important aspect of discipleship. Luke 8 tells us that Mary Magdalene and a number of other women were followers—disciples—of Jesus during his public ministry. And it is these same women who stayed with him during the crucifixion and who were witnesses to the empty tomb.

As we get to know Mary Magdalene (or Mary of Magdala, as she is sometimes called), we will explore the journey of discipleship that brought her to—and from—the empty tomb and that led to her being honored with the title of apostle. We will look at discipleship and apostleship, and at how these terms apply to Mary and to other women of the early church. And we will see, I hope, that these words can be applied to us as well! We, too, are called into a life-changing relationship with the Lord. We, too, are called to be disciples . . . and even apostles!

Called into Discipleship

Begin by asking God to assist you in your prayer and study. Then read through Luke 8:1-8 to be introduced to Mary Magdalene's involvement in Jesus' public ministry.

Luke 8:1-8

[1]Afterward [Jesus] journeyed from one town and village to another, preaching and proclaiming the good news of the kingdom of God. Accompanying him were the Twelve [2]and some women who had been cured of evil spirits and infirmities, Mary, called Magdalene, from whom seven demons had gone out, [3]Joanna, the wife of Herod's steward Chuza, Susanna, and many others who provided for them out of their resources.

[4]When a large crowd gathered, with people from one town after another journeying to him, he spoke in a parable. [5]"A sower went out to sow his seed. And as he sowed, some seed fell on the path and was trampled, and the birds of the sky ate it up. [6]Some seed fell on rocky ground, and when it grew, it withered for lack of moisture. [7]Some seed fell among thorns,

and the thorns grew with it and choked it. [8]And some seed fell on good soil, and when it grew, it produced fruit a hundredfold." After saying this, he called out, "Whoever has ears to hear ought to hear."

After a few moments of quiet reflection on the passage, consider the following background information provided in "Setting the Scene."

Setting the Scene

The gospels give us several stories of the call of particular disciples, of their first encounter with Jesus, but there are many more disciples about whom we are told little or nothing. Jesus seems to have specifically called some people to follow him. There were others, apparently, who chose for themselves to follow this compassionate and charismatic man. Their call came through seeing the things Jesus did and hearing his words; his very presence called out to them. It was through their connection with him, their growing relationship with him and with his followers, that they "heard the call." This number included both men and women.

We know little about Mary Magdalene and the other women who followed Jesus, and even less about what their "following" entailed. But it seems that they were, indeed, disciples: following after him physically and also following his teaching and his example. They were learning from their Master—and that is what a disciple does.

Who was Mary Magdalene?

Who was Mary Magdalene? As is the case with many of the people we read about in the Bible, little of her story is given. Much is left to our imaginations! Often, in my imagination, I have pictured her as a middle-aged woman, a childless widow, a woman of some means, who, when Jesus healed her, responded with heartfelt thanks. Out of gratitude and generosity, she desired to learn from and to follow Jesus, and to support his ministry. And in so doing, she found a place of belonging, a family. She became one of those "who hear the word of God and act on it" (Luke 8:21)—which is how Jesus defines his family later in this chapter. Her new life was one of gratitude and hope. She was growing in love of the Father through Jesus and coming to know herself as part of God's family. Using your imagination to read and pray with Scripture is a practice much encouraged by St. Ignatius, among others. The picture I have given here of Mary Magdalene is simply my picture, my imagination. Others have other ideas. (Perhaps my picture of Mary Magdalene is influenced by my own circumstances: if I had written this when I was in my twenties, my image might have been very different!)

Very little is actually known about Mary Magdalene. Was she a repentant sinner? A reformed prostitute? These images of Mary have stirred hearts and minds for centuries. They are, however, much more gossip than gospel! They are not part of the biblical story of Mary Magdalene. They are part of the confusion and misinformation that have swirled around her over the centuries, clouding her reputation. It owes something to overactive (perhaps we could say artistic or romantic) imaginations and something to a lamentable blending and mixing of her story with those of other women in the gospels. This misunderstanding can be traced back to commentaries from the fourth and fifth centuries. The gospels never portray Mary Magdalene as a prostitute or a sinner.

Instead, the gospels present Mary, quite simply, as a disciple. Luke tells us that she is a woman who has been healed by Jesus and who now follows him and looks after his needs. That's the picture we get from the passage in Luke 8, quoted above. This presentation of Mary Magdalene as a disciple can also be found in the longer ending of Mark's gospel (16:9-20). Both Matthew and Mark, in their passion narratives, also tell us of Mary Magdalene and the other women who followed Jesus and provided for, or ministered to, him (Mark 15; Matt 27). It's a bare-boned description, but it is pretty clearly a description of discipleship.

The passage in Luke 8, introducing Mary and the other women disciples, is followed by the Parable of the Sower, an important teaching on discipleship. Through this parable, Jesus illustrates what it means to say yes to the call to discipleship and to become "fertile ground" for God's word. The meaning of discipleship will be explored more fully as we go along.

The entire passage will be considered a few verses at a time. The questions in the margins are for group discussion or for personal reflection or journaling.

Understanding the Scene Itself

¹**Afterward he journeyed from one town and village to another, preaching and proclaiming the good news of the kingdom of God. Accompanying him were the Twelve** ²**and some women who had been cured of evil spirits and infirmities, Mary, called Magdalene, from whom seven demons had gone out.**

The previous chapter of Luke is filled with encounters between Jesus and various groups of people in the region. At the beginning of Luke 8, we find Jesus on the move. This was his common practice: he was an itinerant preacher. He traveled throughout Galilee, "preaching and proclaiming the good news." He was a man with a purpose, a mission: doing the will of the Father. He was proclaiming the message God had given him to proclaim. We are familiar with much of his preaching and teaching: the beatitudes, the parables, the discourses. He attracted eager crowds, and he taught them that God's mercy and forgiveness were freely available to them. He showed that God was reaching out to them in compassionate love. Jesus taught them that God was calling them into relationship, calling them to live in justice and righteousness. His message of compassion, inclusion, healing, and peace spoke to many. And his words were backed up by his deeds: healings and other miracles, reaching out to and welcoming the poor, the outcast, the marginalized. Many of his listeners—including many women—responded very positively. Many of them accompanied him on his travels and became disciples.

As already noted, we have accounts of apostles like Peter and Andrew, James and John, being called by Jesus and leaving everything to follow him. But for several of the apostles, we have no story of how they came to be followers of Jesus. And we know that, beyond the group of twelve apostles, there was a much larger group of followers—disciples. We don't know if they were called by Jesus or simply chose on their own to follow him. In the passage we are focusing on, from Luke 8, we are told that Jesus, in this particular journey, was accompanied by "the Twelve and some women." Besides Mary, two other women—Joanna and Susanna—are mentioned. We are given very little information about them though, only that they had been cured by Jesus and responded by becoming disciples.

What attracted you to Jesus? How would you sum up his message?

Cured of what? We aren't sure. Of the women in general, Luke says that they "had been cured of evil spirits and infirmities." Speaking of Mary Magdalene, he says that "seven demons" had been driven out of her. From a modern perspective, biblical references to demon possession might be taken to mean any number of illnesses or conditions: epilepsy or seizures, mental or emotional illness, perhaps grief, depression, or what we would now call posttraumatic stress; there are varying explanations. A sinful past might or might not be part of this story of suffering. We have no way of knowing the particulars.

Certainly, in biblical times, illness and suffering were often considered to be the result of sin. And illness carried a stigma that left the sufferer feeling isolated and ashamed. Mary Magdalene would have experienced that. Although we do not know the details of her situation, what we can say with certainty is that she had been suffering greatly and had been healed by Jesus. Her response was one of gratitude and generosity. And this is true of the other women as well.

[3]**Joanna, the wife of Herod's steward Chuza, Susanna, and many others who provided for them out of their resources.**

The final thing Luke tells us in this paragraph about Mary and the other women who followed Jesus and the Twelve is that they "provided for them out of their resources." It seems likely that they were women of some means (we are told that Joanna was "the wife of Herod's steward Chuza," which indicates a position of some status and wealth). We can assume that they provided financial assistance to the apostles and maybe also looked after them in other ways—preparing meals, perhaps. We might wonder if they also reached out to other women who came to hear Jesus, perhaps making them feel welcome, perhaps sharing some of Jesus' teachings with them.

This is not to imply that Jesus had wealthy women as patrons who saw to his every need! That does not fit the image of the Son of Man who had "nowhere to rest his head" (Matt 8:20). Nor does it fit the image of the poor man from Nazareth who identified with and befriended the poor and who spoke strong warnings to those who relied on their riches. But there were people, men and women, who were willing and able to use their material possessions to help Jesus and his mission. And Jesus would benefit from physical nourishment and nurturing on his journey, just as he benefited from the spiritual nourishment that came when he went aside by himself to pray. Those who responded positively to his message wished to support his mission in various ways. Some welcomed him into their homes; some left everything to follow him. Some, it seems, supported him financially.

What women have brought you to Jesus or shared Jesus' teachings with you?

Luke's mention of "the resources" of the women might lead us to focus rather narrowly on financial resources. Current Catholic teaching on stewardship can help to expand our understanding. The term "stewardship" has come to encompass the resources of "time, talent, and treasure." Surely, this wider understanding applies well to Mary and her companions (and it fits with Matthew and Mark's description of the women as "ministering to" Jesus—see Matt 27, treated in the next chapter, or Mark 15:40-41). Mary Magdalene and the other women gave Jesus their time, their talent, and their treasure. Perhaps the talents they were able to offer included traditional domestic talents, like providing meals and accommodations. They also spent time with him, learning from him and serving him. They offered their talents of hospitality and caring, their gifts of compassion and presence.

> What gifts do you have that are being used to spread God's love in the world?

Let's take a deeper look now at Mary Magdalene as a disciple. We can define a disciple as one who follows and, more specifically, as one who learns from a Master. Jesus' disciples followed him literally and figuratively: they traveled with him; they learned from him and modeled their lives on his. They followed his teaching and they followed his example. Meeting Jesus changed their lives. This is true of the Twelve, but it is also true of a much wider group, including the women mentioned in Luke 8.

To our frustration, we are told little about them. Were these women well known in the early church? Did the original gospel audiences already know their stories . . . did they even, perhaps, know some of these women? We wish we knew!

The gospels give us various examples of women who were disciples: not necessarily following Jesus on his journeys, but following his teachings, following his examples, learning from their Master, and living out what they were learning. We can certainly speak of Mary of Nazareth as the first and foremost disciple, who said "yes" to bearing Jesus to the world. And we are told of Martha and Mary, and of the Samaritan woman at the well. It may be that the mother of James and John—the wife of Zebedee—was one of the women who accompanied Jesus on his travels. We know of at least one occasion when she was journeying with him (Matt 20:20), and she was with him at the cross (Matt 27). The number of women disciples may have been relatively small (compared to the number of men), but in such a patriarchal culture, it is surely remarkable that they existed at all!

While it is true that little is said in the gospels about the women followers of Jesus, it is not surprising that his ministry attracted many women. His ministry had great appeal to the marginalized. We know that Jesus had a special connection to the outsider, the poor and lowly. This included "tax collectors and sinners" (see, for example, Mark 2:15); it included foreigners and non-Jews (Matt 8:5ff). It also included women, who, in a patriarchal society, were often marginalized. He called the humble, the neglected, the outcast into community, identity, and belonging.

How does Jesus' reaching out to women show that he reaches out to the marginalized? Have you thought much about the role of women in the early church? What does it mean to you that Jesus welcomed women into discipleship?

Reading the passage from Luke 8 about Mary Magdalene and the other women who followed Jesus reminded me of a passage from Mark's gospel, the passage where Jesus heals Simon Peter's mother-in-law. This is the second miracle recorded in Mark's gospel, still in chapter 1. Following is a quotation from the passage, using the New Revised Standard Version translation: "He came and took her by the hand and lifted her up. Then the fever left her, and she began to serve them" (Mark 1:31). Jesus lifts people up, gives them new life, by raising them to a new understanding of who they are, a new awareness of their value and dignity as children of God. And they respond in gratitude and self-giving. They want to serve him. That's what we see with Simon Peter's mother-in-law. And that's what we see with Mary Magdalene. Jesus brought Mary healing, wholeness, restoration—new life. She responded with generosity and love. As with Simon Peter's mother-in-law, when Mary experienced healing, it led to a desire to serve. She and the other women named in Luke 8, who had also experienced healing, traveled with Jesus and his friends, and "provided for them." The self-giving love of Jesus called forth self-giving love from them.

Mary was healed and responded in gratitude. What has led you to expressions of gratitude?

[4]When a large crowd gathered, with people from one town after another journeying to him, he

spoke in a parable. ⁵"A sower went out to sow his seed. And as he sowed, some seed fell on the path and was trampled, and the birds of the sky ate it up. ⁶Some seed fell on rocky ground, and when it grew, it withered for lack of moisture. ⁷Some seed fell among thorns, and the thorns grew with it and choked it. ⁸And some seed fell on good soil, and when it grew, it produced fruit a hundredfold." After saying this, he called out, "Whoever has ears to hear ought to hear."

Mary and her companions responded to Jesus' outreach to them by becoming disciples. It was his healing and compassionate presence that "called" them to discipleship. In chapter 8, immediately after he tells us of the women who followed Jesus, Luke places the parable of the Sower and the Seed. We can see in these women seed that "fell on good soil, . . . and produced fruit a hundredfold."

"Good soil" is prepared and receptive. It welcomes life and allows life to flourish. Jesus uses this image to describe those who are open to hear and to follow him. The call to be "good soil" is a call into intimacy and community, a shared life: shared with Jesus and with all his brothers and sisters. The journey of discipleship is a shared journey. We learn from and support one another. And always we journey

> **A disciple is one who follows, and learns from, a teacher.**

with—and toward!—Jesus, our teacher, our support, and our guide. Mary and the other women who became disciples followed Jesus with open, grateful hearts and minds eager to learn. They grew and matured together. God's word, deeply rooted in them, would help them to withstand trials and challenges—rocky ground and thorns—as they matured in their commitment and developed hope and courage.

Jesus, in his words and his actions, taught many to see themselves as fertile soil where the seed of God's word will flourish. He taught them that they were known, loved, and valued by God. That is the basis and core of discipleship; everything flows from that. Then Jesus taught his disciples to respond to that love: to respond to the call to lives of service to others, lives of compassion and generosity. This we see in Mary Magdalene. This is a lived discipleship: a responding to the message and the life of Jesus, a modeling of that message and that life. It is learning to abide in God's love. It is a following of Jesus' new commandment: "As I have loved you, so you also should love one another" (John 13:34). Mary and her companions were learning to do what Jesus did, and that's what all disciples are called to do.

Mary Magdalene is an example for us of someone whose life was changed by the Lord

Do you think of yourself as a disciple? What does being a disciple mean to you?

Jesus. Her discipleship "produced fruit a hundredfold." She came to see herself as loved and valued by God. She came to see that she had gifts that could be used in service to God and God's people. She grew in faith and trust because she experienced healing and acceptance from Jesus. She learned from him and modeled her life on his. She was a woman of gratitude and of generosity. She is a wonderful example of what it means to be a Christian disciple, someone we can admire and emulate.

Praying the Word / Sacred Reading

Return to the passage in Luke 8:1-8, reading it carefully and prayerfully. What words or phrases speak to you? Let yourself linger with these words or phrases so that God may speak to you. Try to memorize those particular words or phrases:

- *Write them down.*

- *Use them in your prayer this week.*

- *Let them speak to you about what it means to be a disciple.*

- *Hear in them your call to follow Jesus.*

Spend time praying about your discipleship. Your prayer may include gratitude, repentance, hope, resolve, confusion, questioning. . . . Bring it to the Lord: have a conversation with Jesus about being his disciple.

Living the Word

As you go about your week, be mindful of the women around you. What examples are there in your life of women disciples? What women do you know who are producing "fruit a hundredfold"?

Offer a prayer of thanksgiving for these women, and keep them in your prayer.

Find a way to thank or encourage at least one of the "Mary Magdalenes" in your life.

At the Foot of the Cross

*Begin by asking God to assist you in your prayer
and study. Then read through Matthew 27:45-61,
the portrayal of Jesus' death on the cross and
Mary's presence there.*

Matthew 27:45-61

[45]From noon onward, darkness came over the whole land until
three in the afternoon. [46]And about three o'clock Jesus cried
out in a loud voice, *"Eli, Eli, lema sabachthani?"* which means,
"My God, my God, why have you forsaken me?" [47]Some of the
bystanders who heard it said, "This one is calling for Elijah."
[48]Immediately one of them ran to get a sponge; he soaked it in
wine, and putting it on a reed, gave it to him to drink. [49]But the
rest said, "Wait, let us see if Elijah comes to save him." [50]But
Jesus cried out again in a loud voice, and gave up his spirit.
[51]And behold, the veil of the sanctuary was torn in two from
top to bottom. The earth quaked, rocks were split, [52]tombs were

opened, and the bodies of many saints who had fallen asleep were raised. [53]And coming forth from their tombs after his resurrection, they entered the holy city and appeared to many. [54]The centurion and the men with him who were keeping watch over Jesus feared greatly when they saw the earthquake and all that was happening, and they said, "Truly, this was the Son of God!" [55]There were many women there, looking on from a distance, who had followed Jesus from Galilee, ministering to him. [56]Among them were Mary Magdalene and Mary the mother of James and Joseph, and the mother of the sons of Zebedee.

[57]When it was evening, there came a rich man from Arimathea named Joseph, who was himself a disciple of Jesus. [58]He went to Pilate and asked for the body of Jesus; then Pilate ordered it to be handed over. [59]Taking the body, Joseph wrapped it [in] clean linen [60]and laid it in his new tomb that he had hewn in the rock. Then he rolled a huge stone across the entrance to the tomb and departed. [61]But Mary Magdalene and the other Mary remained sitting there, facing the tomb.

After a few moments of quiet reflection on the passage, consider the following background information provided in "Setting the Scene."

Setting the Scene

Jesus attracted many admiring followers. There were those who flocked to hear his teaching. There were those who were healed and responded in gratitude. But there were many whose reaction to Jesus was very different. There were those who were shocked by some of his actions; many who felt threatened; many who resented his teachings; many who were angry.

In Luke 8, we learned of Mary Magdalene's place among the disciples. If we had moved on to Luke 9, we would have read of Jesus' determination to head toward Jerusalem and of his warnings to his disciples of his approaching suffering and death. We would have heard of difficulties associated with following him: the cost of discipleship. We could find similar passages in the other Synoptic Gospels of Matthew and Mark.

The disciples were unable—or unwilling—to understand Jesus' warnings. They were focusing on the benefits and the joys of following Jesus, on all they were learning, on all they were doing. They weren't ready to see a wider reality. But Jesus could "read the signs of the times," and his pronouncements of danger to come soon were proven true. Not all of his followers coped well as things began to change. Not all of them responded well to the deeper challenges of Jesus' teachings or to the criticisms and threats being raised against him. Some turned away from following him. Surprisingly, many of the women, along with the Twelve and some others, continued to follow and support him.

But when we come to Jesus' arrest, trial, and execution, the gospel picture is very stark. We are shown that he was left virtually alone. The Twelve, overcome with fear and despair, fled. Almost everyone fled. A few women remained.

Mary Magdalene had loyally followed Jesus and served him during his public ministry. When the time of his suffering and death came, she continued to serve him in the only way possible: by her loving and compassionate presence. In Jesus' death, and in the events leading up to it, she and the other women learned one of the great lessons of the paschal mystery: you can't go *around* suffering; you have to go *through* it.

The entire passage will be considered a few verses at a time. The questions in the margins are for discussion with others. If you are using these materials on your own, use the questions for personal reflection or as a guide for journaling.

Understanding the Scene Itself

[45]From noon onward, darkness came over the whole land until three in the afternoon. [46]And about three o'clock Jesus cried out in a loud voice, *"Eli, Eli, lema sabachthani?"* which means, "My God, my God, why have you forsaken me?" [47]Some of the bystanders who heard it said, "This one is calling for Elijah." [48]Immediately one of them ran to get a sponge; he soaked it in wine, and putting it on a reed, gave it to him to drink. [49]But the rest said, "Wait, let us see if Elijah comes to save him." [50]But Jesus cried out again in a loud voice, and gave up his spirit. [51]And behold, the veil of the sanctuary was torn in two from top to bottom. The earth quaked, rocks were split, [52]tombs were opened, and the bodies of many saints who had fallen

asleep were raised. [53]And coming forth from their tombs after his resurrection, they entered the holy city and appeared to many.

The church teaches us that Jesus is fully human and fully divine. And we see the fullness of his humanity in the passion narratives. We see that he, like every person who has ever lived, knows the reality of pain and suffering, of fear and sadness, of loneliness and despair. We see clearly that Jesus fully accepts what it is to be human . . . even accepting death.

In the passion narratives, we see the worst of humanity: we see cruelty and violence; we see betrayal and abandonment. We see fear and weakness. And we see Jesus, the model of loyal commitment to God and to God's purpose. We see Jesus, the model of humble obedience and humble suffering.

As we observe Jesus in his great suffering and powerlessness, we see, too, the helplessness and hopelessness of those around him. In Matthew's

telling of the story, Jesus cries out: "My God, my God, why have you forsaken me?" And creation itself mirrors his pain and isolation: "darkness came over the whole land . . . [t]he earth quaked, rocks were split . . ."

The signs that accompany the death of Jesus arouse fear and awe. They reflect the crucifixion, but they also prefigure the resurrection. The veil of the temple is torn in two, symbolizing a new access to God, a tearing down of all that divides God and humanity. In addition to the signs of darkness and earthquakes, there is another sign: graves are opened "and the bodies of many saints who had fallen asleep were raised." In the midst of his description of the crucifixion, Matthew points us ahead to the resurrection, telling us: "And coming forth from their tombs after his resurrection, they entered the holy city and appeared to many."

Crucifixion and resurrection are that closely connected: crucifixion leads to resurrection. This was so for Jesus, and it is so for those he loves. That's what Matthew teaches us in speaking of "the bodies of many saints": what was true for Jesus is true for his followers. This is our faith; this is the source of our hope. But it is a two-sided coin, a double-edged sword: death and resurrection. That is the pattern for Jesus; that is the pattern for us. It is the paschal mystery: death and new life. We reach new life by going through death. We can't get around it. We have to go through it. There is no other way.

But this is a hard lesson . . . so painfully, frightfully hard. Who is ready? Who is prepared?

What experiences have shown you the close connection between crucifixion and resurrection? Between death and life?

Though Jesus tried to teach his followers, tried to prepare them for what was to come, it is no wonder, really, that they did not understand, that they were not prepared.

We naturally back away from the reality of death. We back away from suffering. We want to avoid them at any cost. We fear change; we fear the unknown, especially death. We find it so hard to accept that pain and suffering—even death—can have any benefit, any purpose, that they can lead to new life. But this is a teaching Jesus insists we have to learn.

[54]The centurion and the men with him who were keeping watch over Jesus feared greatly when they saw the earthquake and all that was happening, and they said, "Truly, this was the Son of God!" [55]There were many women there, looking on from a distance, who had followed Jesus from Galilee, ministering to him. [56]Among them were Mary Magdalene and Mary the mother of James and Joseph, and the mother of the sons of Zebedee.

Even in fear and anguish, there were some who stayed near . . . as close as they could. Perhaps it was easier for the women. In this patriarchal culture, perhaps it was possible for them to stay near and still be more or less unnoticed. Women were seen as less significant, less important—certainly less of a threat. So, less attention might have been paid to them than to Jesus' male disciples.

This is not to say that it would have been easy for them. Not at all. We should never try to downplay their misery or their fear. We applaud their compassion, their courage, and their loyalty. We can recognize their empathy too, for they were people who had suffered themselves: these women had been healed by Jesus. We may not know exactly what the gospel writers are signifying when they tell us that Mary Magdalene was healed of seven demons, but we can be sure that it was a release from a great deal of suffering. And so, now, Mary and her companions stayed near to the one who had healed their suffering, supporting him in his suffering. It was their love and compassion that overcame their fear and kept them near to Jesus in his suffering and his death.

When has compassion helped you to overcome fear?

We can imagine their compassion was not only for Jesus, but also for one another. They supported each other in their misery and their fear. This band of women, little known, little noticed, stood together in love and solidarity. Since Mary Magdalene's name generally leads the list of women disciples, perhaps she was seen by the other women as a leader. Perhaps they were accustomed to look to her for teaching and guidance, valuing the wisdom of her experience and the compassion and empathy she had developed. And so, they would value her presence now, as they gathered together in shared sorrow. This was a coming together of motherly hearts,

When have you experienced the sharing of grief? How might this recollection help you to imagine the grief of the women at Jesus' death?

united in grief. Mary Magdalene was there through it all—with Jesus, with his mother, with the other women—keeping vigil together.

Mark 15:40-41 tells us there was a group of women keeping watch as Jesus died on the cross. Mark portrays them as disciples, saying that they "had followed him when he was in Galilee and ministered to him," echoing what we have already learned from Luke 8. Matthew's passion account names three of the women: "Mary Magdalene and Mary the mother of James and Joseph, and the mother of the sons of Zebedee" (Matt 27:56). Each of the four evangelists gives a slightly different listing of the women who stayed near the cross of Jesus. Mark lists Mary Magdalene, Mary the mother of James and of Joses, and Salome. Luke simply mentions "the women who had followed him from Galilee" (Luke 23:49). And John tells us of "[Jesus'] mother and his mother's sister, Mary the wife of Clopas, and Mary of Magdala" (John 19:25). The lists vary, but each evangelist remembers that women remained steadfast, staying near to Jesus as he died.

⁵⁷**When it was evening, there came a rich man from Arimathea named Joseph, who was himself a disciple of Jesus. ⁵⁸He went to Pilate and asked for the body of Jesus; then Pilate ordered it to**

be handed over. [59]Taking the body, Joseph wrapped it [in] clean linen [60]and laid it in his new tomb that he had hewn in the rock. Then he rolled a huge stone across the entrance to the tomb and departed. [61]But Mary Magdalene and the other Mary remained sitting there, facing the tomb.

Not all of Jesus' male disciples fled. There are differences in how each evangelist tells the story, but the name of Joseph of Arimathea is remembered in each account. Matthew tells us that Joseph took the body, wrapped it in a burial shroud, and laid it in his own tomb. Then Matthew closes out his scene by returning to the women, who had remained and watched all that happened. Mary Magdalene and the other Mary, Matthew tells us, "remained sitting there, facing the tomb."

We are left with an image of Mary Magdalene, loyal and committed to the end, sitting in her grief, no doubt overwhelmed with shock and sorrow and fear, but still staying near. Keeping vigil.

Can you think of times when a simple presence has been more important than words?

Praying the Word / Sacred Reading

Return to the passage in Matthew 27:45-61, reading it carefully and prayerfully. Use your imagination now and put yourself in the scene.

- *Be with Mary Magdalene and Jesus' other disciples in their grief and fear. Use all your senses to enter into the scene. What do you see, hear, feel? Ask God to open your heart to new perspectives on this well-known scene.*

- *Then spend some time journaling or discussing with others: What insights have you gained from spending time with Mary Magdalene at the foot of the cross? Take these insights back to God in a quiet time of prayer.*

Living the Word

We have pictured Mary and the other women at the cross, united in their sorrow, supporting one another in pain and grief. There are many ways we can support one another in sorrow and suffering. Find out more about what your parish or diocese, or your city or region, is doing to support those who are suffering. Grief support groups or hospice care might be examples, but there are many other forms of support.

Are there ways you could get involved? Ways you can support these movements? Your response may be physical; it may be financial; it may be a response of learning more, or of prayer and intercession.

In your prayers, include ministries to those who suffer. Remember, too, times that you have kept vigil. Reflect on these times and bring to God those you know, or those around you, who are currently keeping vigil in some way. Pray for those who are dying or grieving. Recognize that you are connected to them in the Body of Christ.

On Easter Morning

Begin by asking God to assist you in your prayer and study. Then read through John 20:1-18, the story of Mary Magdalene on Easter morning.

John 20:1-18

[1]On the first day of the week, Mary of Magdala came to the tomb early in the morning, while it was still dark, and saw the stone removed from the tomb. [2]So she ran and went to Simon Peter and to the other disciple whom Jesus loved, and told them, "They have taken the Lord from the tomb, and we don't know where they put him." [3]So Peter and the other disciple went out and came to the tomb. [4]They both ran, but the other disciple ran faster than Peter and arrived at the tomb

first; [5]he bent down and saw the burial cloths there, but did not go in. [6]When Simon Peter arrived after him, he went into the tomb and saw the burial cloths there, [7]and the cloth that had covered his head, not with the burial cloths but rolled up in a separate place. [8]Then the other disciple also went in, the one who had arrived at the tomb first, and he saw and believed. [9]For they did not yet understand the scripture that he had to rise from the dead. [10]Then the disciples returned home.

[11]But Mary stayed outside the tomb weeping. And as she wept, she bent over into the tomb [12]and saw two angels in white sitting there, one at the head and one at the feet where the body of Jesus had been. [13]And they said to her, "Woman, why are you weeping?" She said to them, "They have taken my Lord, and I don't know where they laid him." [14]When she had said this, she turned around and saw Jesus there, but did not know it was Jesus. [15]Jesus said to her, "Woman, why are you weeping? Whom are you looking for?" She thought it was the gardener and said to him, "Sir, if you carried him away, tell me where you laid him, and I will take him." [16]Jesus said to her, "Mary!" She turned and said to him in Hebrew, "Rabbouni," which means Teacher. [17]Jesus said to her, "Stop holding on to me, for I have not yet ascended to the Father. But go to my brothers and tell them, 'I am going to my Father and your Father, to my God and your God.'" [18]Mary of Magdala went and announced to the disciples, "I have seen the Lord," and what he told her.

After a few moments of quiet reflection on the passage, consider the following background information provided in "Setting the Scene."

Setting the Scene

As we approach the end of our study, we return to something mentioned near the beginning: Mary Magdalene as "the apostle to the apostles." It is her announcement of the Easter message that earns her that title, and so we turn now to the story of Mary Magdalene on Easter morning.

There are varying accounts of the Easter witnesses in the four gospels. Mary Magdalene is mentioned in each gospel. It is John's account that gives special attention to her role after the resurrection.

Jesus had healed her and called her to newness of life. She had traveled with him throughout Galilee and on to Jerusalem. She had learned from him and supported him. She had cared for him and committed her life to him. She had found meaning and purpose in her life with him. She had stood by him in his agony and death. She had loved and suffered and grieved. She had watched and waited as he was laid in the tomb. Then she rested on the Sabbath, as the Law required. And as soon as she could, she returned to the tomb, to be near her Master and to mourn. But the tomb was not as she had left it. It was open, and empty. And her whole world was about to change.

Understanding the Scene Itself

[1]On the first day of the week, Mary of Magdala came to the tomb early in the morning, while it was still dark, and saw the stone removed from the tomb. [2]So she ran and went to Simon Peter and to the other disciple whom Jesus loved, and told them, "They have taken the Lord from the tomb, and we don't know where they put him." [3]So Peter and the other disciple went out and came to the tomb. [4]They both ran, but the other disciple ran faster than Peter and arrived at the tomb first; [5]he bent down and saw the burial cloths there, but did not go in. [6]When Simon Peter arrived after him, he went into the tomb and saw the burial cloths there, [7]and the cloth that had covered his head, not with the burial cloths but rolled up in a separate place. [8]Then the other disciple also went in, the one who had arrived at the tomb first, and he saw and believed. [9]For they did not yet understand the scripture that he had to rise from the dead. [10]Then the disciples returned home.

Chapter 20 of John's gospel opens on a scene of darkness and emptiness. We are presented with Mary Magdalene (apparently alone) facing

the darkness and emptiness of grief, fear, and lack of understanding. And now facing an empty tomb. She has come to be near the body of Jesus, to mourn, perhaps to pray, but she is confronted with something unexpected, something she can't understand. The tomb is open; the stone has been rolled away. The body of Jesus is not inside. She doesn't know what this means, but she fears the worst: the Master's body has been stolen.

So she hurries to Simon Peter and the Beloved Disciple to report this to them. Her words to them imply that she was not alone at the tomb: "They have taken the Lord from the tomb, and we don't know where they put him." The other gospels mention a group of women going to the tomb on Easter morning. Mary's use of the word "we" implies that others had gone to the tomb with her, but the Fourth Evangelist has chosen to focus solely on Mary Magdalene. Her shock and grief cause Peter and his unnamed companion to hurry to the tomb, to see for themselves.

When you are confused or in crisis, whom do you turn to? And what do you hope to receive from them?

The sense of urgency among Jesus' followers dominates these verses.

The "Beloved Disciple" appears several times in the Fourth Gospel, always anonymous, always intimately close and lovingly connected to Jesus. In this, the Beloved Disciple is an example of what the perfect disciple should be. We hear now that the Beloved Disciple allows Peter to enter the tomb first, respecting Peter's leadership status among the apostles. But it is Peter's companion who first grasps what has happened. We are told that the Beloved Disciple "saw and believed." We are not told how or why; we get no more of the story of Peter and his companion at this point. Without seeing the risen Lord, and with only a limited understanding of what has happened, the two return home. Mary Magdalene stays behind.

> What are some times in your life when you have "stayed behind," feeling unable to move forward?

¹¹**But Mary stayed outside the tomb weeping. And as she wept, she bent over into the tomb ¹²and saw two angels in white sitting there, one at the head and one at the feet where the body of Jesus had been. ¹³And they said to her, "Woman, why are you weeping?" She said to them, "They have taken my Lord, and I don't know where they laid him." ¹⁴When she had said this, she turned around and saw Jesus there, but did not know it was Jesus. ¹⁵Jesus said to her, "Woman, why are you weeping? Whom are you looking for?" She thought it was the gardener and said to him, "Sir, if you carried him away, tell me where you laid him, and I will take him." ¹⁶Jesus said to her, "Mary!" She turned and said**

to him in Hebrew, "Rabbouni," which means Teacher. [17]Jesus said to her, "Stop holding on to me, for I have not yet ascended to the Father. But go to my brothers and tell them, 'I am going to my Father and your Father, to my God and your God.' " [18]Mary of Magdala went and announced to the disciples, "I have seen the Lord," and what he told her.

Mary Magdalene, alone again at the empty tomb, is still without understanding or belief. She has nothing but grief and emptiness. She stands by the tomb and weeps. She is confronted by a vision of angels, but their presence means nothing to her; she cannot get beyond her grief. Then she is confronted by the presence of Jesus himself. Her grief keeps her blind and deaf. She cannot see him for who he is, or even recognize his voice. She is fixated on one idea: the Master's body has been stolen. She asks the "stranger" in front of her—thinking that he is the gardener, who looks after the garden where the tomb was located—if he has taken the body away.

Jesus responds very simply and gently, by saying her name: "Mary!" Then, suddenly, she hears; she sees; she knows. (This sudden awareness is very similar to what happens to the two disciples at the table in Emmaus, in another Easter story, told in the Gospel of Luke, chapter 24.)

In what ways can you relate to Mary's experience of grief, which kept her closed off from everything else?

When have you recognized God's voice in your life?

Quickly and unexpectedly, Mary is plunged from darkness to light, from death to life, from grief to joy. In a split second, everything has changed. This is a sudden seeing, a sudden understanding, deep and visceral: an opening of eyes and heart. It is an immediate grasping, not of all the details, but of the essentials. It is like a conversion experience—like Paul on the road to Damascus (Acts 9). In her original encounter with Jesus and her call into relationship, Mary had already experienced conversion and new life. Easter Sunday builds on that and brings it to a new level. And it is startling and dramatic. Mary has suddenly encountered the risen Lord and the experience has changed her life. She is confronted with a new and shocking knowledge, knowledge that is not completely understood. It is bewildering and confusing as well as awesome and joyful.

It's a lot to take in! Her immediate response is to cling, to stop here, to stay here . . . to rest and remain in this moment of joy. But Jesus tells her not to cling. Instead, he gives her a commission; he sends her on a mission. He authorizes her to be the apostle to the apostles—he appoints her as an evangelist, who will deliver the good news of the resurrection to his other followers.

Mary Magdalene becomes an apostle: one sent out and entrusted with a message. And her message is the good news of the Lord's resurrection, making her also an evangelist (from the

When have you known joy that couldn't be contained and had to share it?

I have seen the Lord!

Greek *evangelion*, "good news"). She returns to Jesus' disciples and proclaims: "I have seen the Lord!"

We generally use the word "apostle" in a narrow sense, meaning the Twelve—Jesus' inner circle, we might say. But the word can have a wider application. In the Acts of the Apostles, Luke reports that, after the death of Judas, the eleven remaining apostles were anxious to restore their number to twelve. A speech from Peter gives the criteria for choosing a replacement for Judas: someone who had "accompanied us the whole time the Lord Jesus came and went among us, beginning from the baptism of John until the day on which he was taken up from us, [must] become with us a witness to his resurrection" (Acts 1:21-22). Matthias is chosen to join the Twelve, but it seems likely that a number of people from the larger group of Jesus' disciples could have qualified as witnesses to Jesus' public ministry, his death, and his resurrection—including Mary Magdalene. This larger group of witnesses and followers might be considered "small a" apostles, for they, too, would be sent out to proclaim the good news of Jesus Christ.

An apostle is sent out to represent the sender, in the sender's name and with the sender's authority. An apostle, then, should know the sender

What experiences have made you say, "I have seen the Lord!"?

How have you been sent or commissioned?

well, should be intimately connected to the sender. This is what we see in the Twelve. It is also what we see in Mary Magdalene. Mary had been with Jesus during his public ministry. She had learned from him, loved him, and served him. And she had been with him during his suffering and death. Now, she has witnessed his glory. Mary Magdalene was truly close to Jesus and knew him well. Her discipleship had grown and flourished throughout his public ministry and through all that followed. She was a worthy candidate to represent him as an apostle, testifying to his resurrection.

Saint Paul, who was not one of the Twelve—who, in fact, had never been a disciple of Jesus of Nazareth or a witness to his death—still considered himself an apostle (see, for example, Rom 1:1). And he extended the title of apostle to others, including his kinswoman Junia (Rom 16:7). Like Paul and Junia (and many others), Mary had been called and chosen by the risen Lord, gifted and commissioned by him to proclaim the good news of the resurrection. And her commission preceded theirs. She was to be the advance guard. This lowly and obscure woman was chosen to go to the apostles, to Jesus' closest companions, and to bring them the news that the Lord was risen. As we see so often, our God is a God of surprises, who chooses the humble, strengthens the weak, and affirms the lowly.

Mary Magdalene became the first of a new people: Easter people. Her experience that Sunday morning changed who she was. This special Easter experience was a straddling of both time

and eternity. It brought her to the other side of the paschal mystery. She had already experienced the cross. . . . Now she had experienced the truth of the resurrection. And she would continue to live in that resurrection faith. It would not take away sadness and suffering from her life, but it would give all things meaning and purpose. It would give all of life hope and joy.

What brings hope and joy to your life?

Mary Magdalene became the first of a long line of Easter people, alleluia people. We, too, are Easter people. We, too, can encounter the risen Lord in the gardens of our everyday lives. We, too, are called by him into new life, into discipleship. Easter Sunday has dawned for us too. The light of the resurrection shines on us, as it shone on Mary.

Mary Magdalene represents all the little-known and unknown members of the communion of saints. She is but one of a host of biblical women and men about whom little is written and little is known. But that doesn't mean that she (or any of them) is unimportant—to God, or to us. She is one of the great cloud of witnesses.

Knowing just a little of the stories of our ancestors in the faith helps us to see that we too, have a story; that we, too, are called into relationship with the Lord; that we, too, are uniquely known and gifted by our Lord . . . even if our lives seem small, obscure, humble, ordinary. Ordinary, humble people: truly this is the makeup of the communion of saints, the Body of Christ. Mary Magdalene and all her humble and little-known sisters and brothers can inspire and encourage us. No doubt they pray for us and support us. They beckon us forward and strengthen us on the journey of faith. They show us that we, too, can live as disciples and as apostles. They help us see that we, too, are Easter people, uniquely called and gifted to live out and to share the good news.

Like Mary Magdalene, we have been called into relationship with the risen Lord. We can know his presence in our lives, and that relationship can grow and deepen, into eternity. We can know his love and rely on his guidance and support, now and forever. Our lives can bear witness to this reality. Like Mary Magdalene, each one of us can say, "I have seen the Lord!"

> In what ways have you been an apostle, bringing the good news of Jesus to others?

Praying the Word / Sacred Reading

Return to the passage in John 20:1-18, reading it carefully and prayerfully. What words or phrases especially attract your attention? Let yourself linger with these words or phrases so that God may speak to you.

- *Try to imagine that you are reading this passage for the first time; try to experience its freshness and surprise. How does it call you to newness of life?*

- *As you reflect and pray with this passage, can you hear yourself being commissioned by the risen Lord as an apostle?*

Living the Word

Look around your parish or your neighborhood.

- *Where have you encountered Easter people?*

- *Where have you encountered signs of new life?*

- *Make a gratitude list. Perhaps you can put it on your fridge or on your bathroom mirror. Or post it on Facebook.*

- *You might want to keep a gratitude journal, adding to it all this week.*

Focus on the Easter people and Easter moments in your life: the people, places, and things that are particularly life-giving for you.

You can also include ways you've been an Easter person or an apostle for others. Gratefully acknowledge how you have been able to bring newness of life to those around you. Gratefully acknowledge the many ways you have been gifted with newness of life.

A Concluding Note

In recognition of Mary Magdalene's stature as an apostle, Pope Francis has elevated the day that honors her (July 22) to the rank of feast. According to the Congregation for Divine Worship:

> [I]t is right that the liturgical celebration of this woman should have the same rank of Feast as that given to the celebration of the Apostles in the General Roman Calendar and that the special mission of this woman should be underlined.

In its 2016 report on the elevated feast day for Mary Magdalene, the Congregation quotes from esteemed sources—such as Thomas Aquinas—honoring Mary as "the apostle to the apostles":

> [S]he becomes an evangelist, that is, a messenger who announces the Good News of the Lord's resurrection or, as Rabanus Maurus and Saint Thomas Aquinas say, she becomes the "apostolorum apostola" because she announces to the apostles what in turn they will announce to the whole world.

St. Mary Magdalene, disciple and apostle . . . pray for us!